BIG BUGS

written by Mary Gribbin
illustrated by Andrew Tewson

Ladybird

Words in **bold** are explained
in the glossary.

Ladybird books are widely available, but in case of
difficulty may be ordered by post or telephone from:

Ladybird Books – Cash Sales Department
Littlegate Road Paignton Devon TQ3 3BE
Telephone 01803 554761

A catalogue record for this book is available
from the British Library

Published by Ladybird Books Ltd Loughborough Leicestershire UK
Ladybird Books Inc Auburn Maine 04210 USA

BIG BUGS

Contents

Goliath Beetle

Goliath beetles are the heaviest beetles in the world. They can weigh as much as 100 grams, which is as heavy as a banana.

Goliath beetles live in the tropical **rain forests** of Africa where it is very hot and damp. Goliath beetles eat pollen, fruit and **sap** from trees. Farmers do not like these beetles because they sometimes eat the crops and cause a lot of damage.

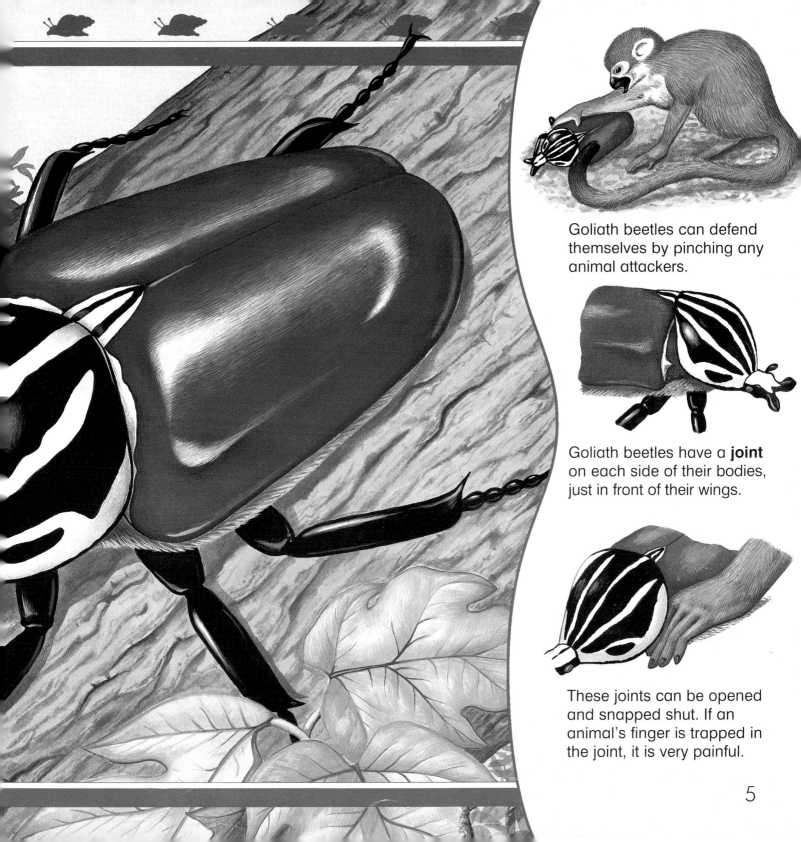

Goliath beetles can defend themselves by pinching any animal attackers.

Goliath beetles have a **joint** on each side of their bodies, just in front of their wings.

These joints can be opened and snapped shut. If an animal's finger is trapped in the joint, it is very painful.

The horns on Hercules beetles' heads can be longer than the beetles' bodies.

When two Hercules beetles fight, they use their horns to push the other beetle over.

Smaller Hercules beetles are more nimble and so usually win the battle!

Hercules Beetle

Hercules beetles are the biggest beetles in the world and live in Central America. They grow to be twenty centimetres long, larger than a small mouse.

Hercules beetles' heads and bodies are protected by a hard casing. Hercules beetles are **nocturnal** creatures. They hunt and feed at night.

Velvet Worm

Velvet worms have long boneless bodies that can fold up like a **concertina**.

To squeeze through a small space, velvet worms make themselves long and thin like a piece of stretched elastic.

Once velvet worms have squeezed through, they go back to their normal shape.

Velvet worms have hundreds of **bristles** all over their bodies, which make these worms look soft and smooth. Velvet worms grow as long as fifteen centimetres, which is about the same size as a carrot. They have

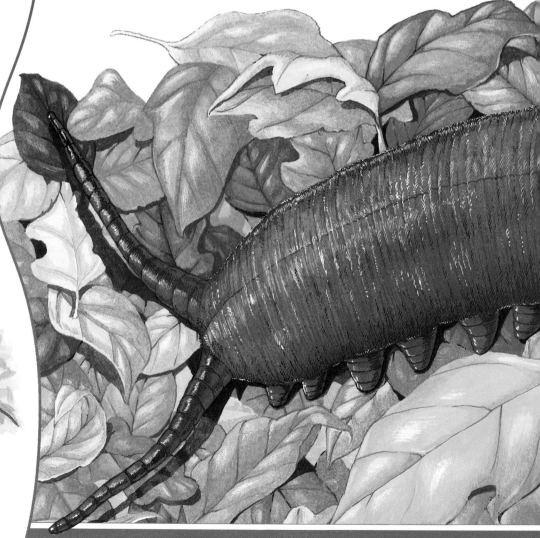

between fourteen and twenty-three pairs of legs. Velvet worms live in South America where they eat other worms and insects. If threatened, velvet worms squirt a sticky liquid all over their attackers.

African Giant Snail

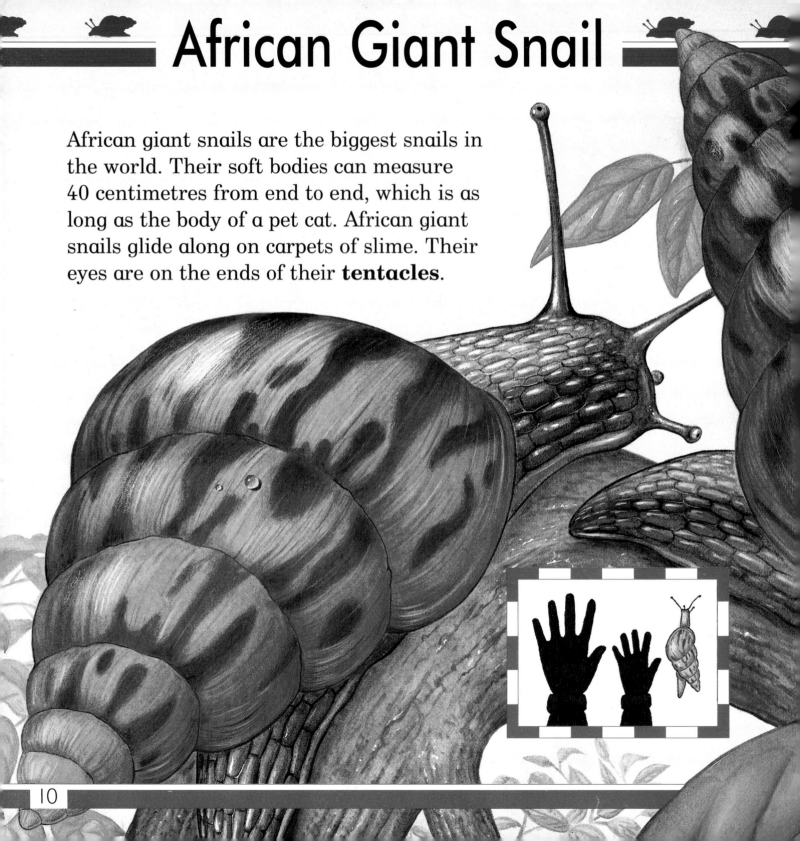

African giant snails are the biggest snails in the world. Their soft bodies can measure 40 centimetres from end to end, which is as long as the body of a pet cat. African giant snails glide along on carpets of slime. Their eyes are on the ends of their **tentacles**.

African giant snails feed on fruit and leaves. They also eat animal bones, which strengthen the snails' shells.

Snails move by sliding along on one broad foot.

A trail of slime oozes out from under the foot. This helps snails glide along.

11

As centipedes grow, their skin does not stretch.

Centipedes become too big for their skin and grow a new one underneath. The old skin splits around the centipedes' heads.

Centipedes wriggle out in their new skin and leave the old one behind.

Giant Centipede

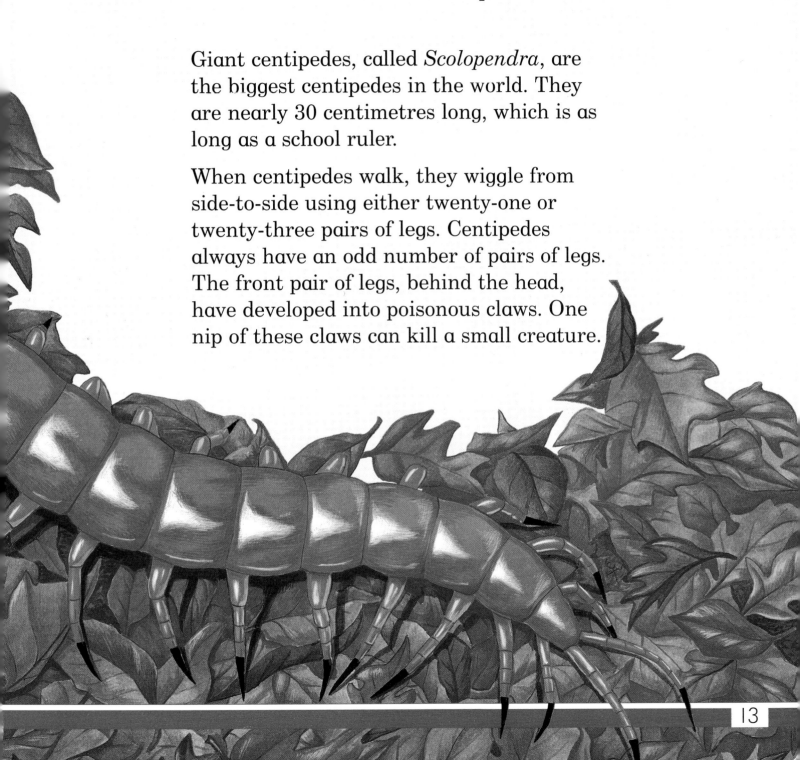

Giant centipedes, called *Scolopendra*, are the biggest centipedes in the world. They are nearly 30 centimetres long, which is as long as a school ruler.

When centipedes walk, they wiggle from side-to-side using either twenty-one or twenty-three pairs of legs. Centipedes always have an odd number of pairs of legs. The front pair of legs, behind the head, have developed into poisonous claws. One nip of these claws can kill a small creature.

Stick Insect

There are about 2,500 different types of stick insect. Most of them live in tropical rain forests where there are lots of trees and bushes. Stick insects are the longest insects in the world and their bodies can be as long as a person's foot. Most stick insects live on branches and are **camouflaged** to look like long, thin twigs.

Some birds or animals like to eat stick insects.

When stick insects are frightened they stay very still on a branch and so they are difficult to see.

Birds think the stick insects are twigs and fly off, leaving the stick insects safe.

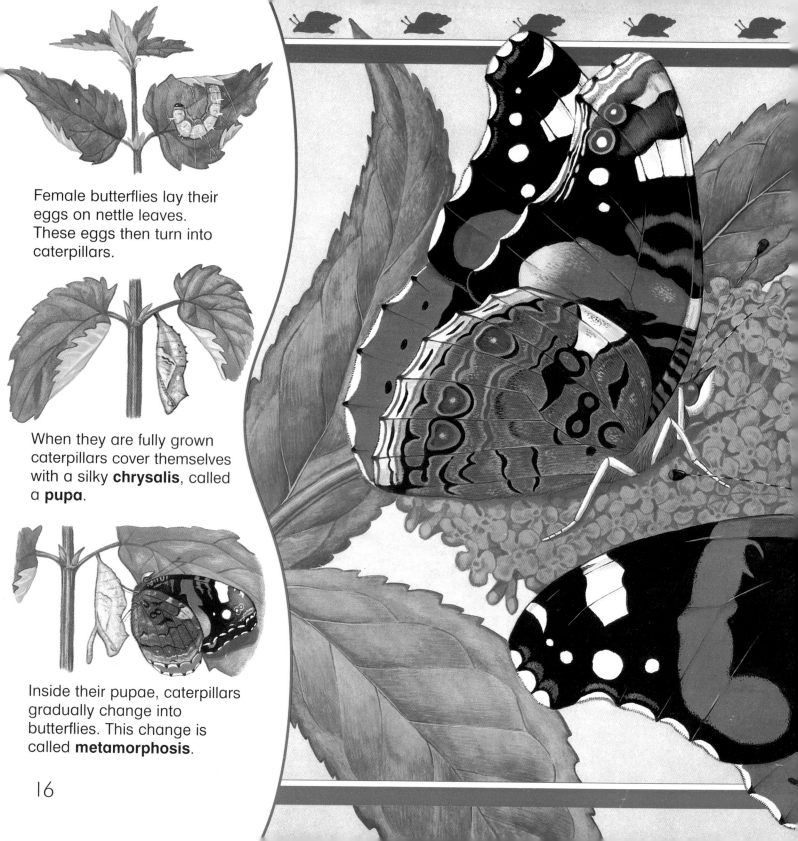

Female butterflies lay their eggs on nettle leaves. These eggs then turn into caterpillars.

When they are fully grown caterpillars cover themselves with a silky **chrysalis**, called a **pupa**.

Inside their pupae, caterpillars gradually change into butterflies. This change is called **metamorphosis**.

16

Red Admiral Butterfly

Red admiral butterflies live in Europe and fly long distances across this continent. Red admiral butterflies do not have teeth and so they can only suck up liquids.

Red admiral butterflies drink **nectar** from flowers, the juice from rotting fruit, and tree sap. They keep their tongues curled up, but uncurl them when feeding.

Tarantula

Tarantulas are the biggest spiders in the world. Some tarantulas that live in South America are as big as dinner plates. Other tarantulas live in trees, and catch small birds to eat.

Tarantulas have special hairs on their feet which act like sticky pads. These hairs help spiders to walk safely over leaves without falling off.

During the day tarantulas rest inside their underground burrows.

At night tarantulas hunt for insects, frogs, mice and small birds.

Tarantulas kill **prey** by biting with their two hollow **fangs**. Poison is injected through the fangs into the victim's body.

Jumping Spider

When insects settle, jumping spiders watch them carefully.

To stop themselves from falling when jumping, these spiders attach themselves to the place they jump from by spinning a strong thread.

Jumping spiders leap onto their victim and bite it with their poisonous fangs.

Jumping spiders are the world's biggest family of spiders. Jumping spiders live on the ground. They have four small eyes at the front of their heads, which help them to spot insects.

Zebra jumping spiders get their name because they are striped and they can jump a long way – more than thirty times their own length.

Fascinating Facts

Goliath Beetle
The wingspan of Goliath beetles measures 25 centimetres, which is as wide as a dinner plate.

Hercules Beetle
Hercules beetles' horns have orange hairs on the inside.

Velvet Worm
Velvet worms do not lay eggs. The young worms grow inside their mother's body.

African Giant Snail
African giant snails can reproduce very quickly. One snail could produce a family of 11 million snails in five years.

Giant Centipede
The name 'centipede' means one hundred legs, but some centipedes can have up to 177 pairs of legs.

Stick Insect
Stick insects' eggs often look like seeds. This hides the eggs from creatures which might eat them.

Red Admiral Butterfly
Each summer, red admiral butterflies fly across the sea from the continent to England. They may then travel on, hundreds of miles, northwards.

Tarantula
Tarantulas defend themselves by rubbing their back legs on their bodies. This sends up a cloud of tiny irritating hairs that can blind an attacker.

Jumping Spider
There are more than 2,800 different types of jumping spider in the world.

Glossary

Bristle A spiky hair which may protect an insect from being eaten or attacked.

Camouflage The way in which animals can avoid being seen, using their colour or shape.

Chrysalis The covering that a caterpillar makes to hide in, while it changes into a moth or butterfly.

Concertina An instrument which folds up into a zigzag.

Fang A sharp tooth which gives a painful prick.

Joint A hinge which joins two parts of a skeleton together.

Metamorphosis The way in which an animal changes form. For example, a caterpillar changes into a butterfly.

Nectar Sweet, sugary water produced by flowers, which attracts insects to the flowers.

Nocturnal The lifestyle of an animal that sleeps during the day and wakes up at night.

Prey Animals which are eaten by other animals for food.

Pupa The last stage in the life of a caterpillar, before it becomes a butterfly or moth.

Rain forest Hot, wet part of the world where trees and plants grow, and many creatures live.

Sap The juice in a plant's stem which some animals drink.

Tentacle A part of the body which sticks out like an arm. A tentacle is used to catch food and can be pulled back into the body.

Index

Comparative sizes

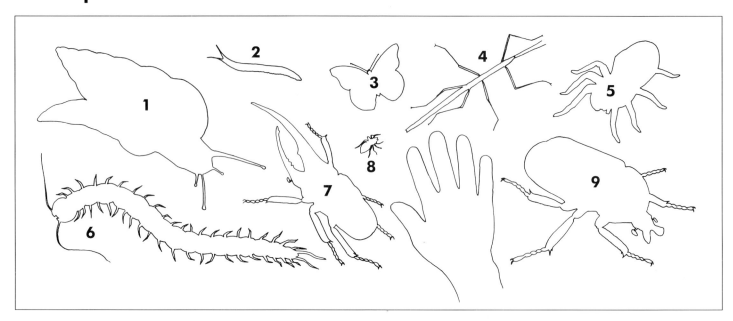

1 African Giant Snail

The biggest snail ever found was an African giant snail that weighed 900 grams which is as heavy as a bag of sugar.

2 Velvet Worm

Small velvet worms are about two-and-a-half centimetres long – as long as a baby's finger.

3 Red Admiral Butterfly

Some red admirals have been known to fly the huge distance across the Atlantic Ocean in twelve days.

4 Stick Insect

The largest stick insects can be found in the tropics. Some stick insects are more than thirty centimetres in length which is almost as long as a person's foot.

5 Tarantula

Tarantulas can weigh as much as 120 grams, which is equivalent to half a pack of butter.

6 Giant Centipede

The bodies of giant centipedes grow to be almost two-and-a-half centimetres wide. This is as wide as a large sausage.

7 Hercules Beetle

The horns of the male Hercules beetles can be longer than their bodies.

8 Zebra Jumping Spider

Some jumping spiders are only five millimetres long which is the size of a drawing pin.

9 Goliath Beetle

This insect may be over ten centimetres long which is as big as a person's fist.

Compare the real size
of these insects with
the size of your hand.